UNPRECEDENTED

UNPRECEDENTED

Ronald L. Faust

RESOURCE *Publications* • Eugene, Oregon

UNPRECEDENTED

Copyright © 2021 Ronald L. Faust. All rights reserved. Except for brief quotations in critical publications or reviews, no part of this book may be reproduced in any manner without prior written permission from the publisher. Write: Permissions, Wipf and Stock Publishers, 199 W. 8th Ave., Suite 3, Eugene, OR 97401.

Resource Publications
An Imprint of Wipf and Stock Publishers
199 W. 8th Ave., Suite 3
Eugene, OR 97401

www.wipfandstock.com

PAPERBACK ISBN: 978-1-7252-9579-7
HARDCOVER ISBN: 978-1-7252-9578-0
EBOOK ISBN: 978-1-7252-9580-3

05/28/21

"Ron shines an uplifting light of wit and wisdom as we slog with him through the mud of meanness and misery. He calls on us to act together to cleanse our world and offers his reckonings as inspiration for the compassion, creativity, and critical thinking essential for this massive mission. As a bonus, Ron breathes hope into the possibilities."

—**CHERI AVERY BLACK**
Author of *Loving to be WE*

"Ron plucks twenty-six letters from the tree of confusion and lets them tumble about with gasps and groans in search of sanity. Wandering gives way to wondering. Suddenly, they twirl and line up to face us, linking hands in poetic protest. As they march straight toward clarity, I swear one of them winks, another flashes a kazoo."

—**KRISS AVERY**
Filmmaker, Rainbow Sound

"*Unprecedented* is informative and imaginative, truth-telling and biting. I highly recommend it!"

—**HENRY M. STOEVER**
Co-chair, PeaceWorks Kansas City, and lawyer advocate

"Ron's works have the rare quality of being both meditative and 'actional.' He is one of the few authors that can bring me from 'zero to street action' in sixty seconds."

—**CHARLES CARNEY**
Retired social worker and director, Compassionate Ministries

"The author reveals his ability to capture the essence of complex problems and offers creative ways of understanding them."

—**JONNE AVERY LONG**
Retired national trainer, Prisoner Visitation and Support

"The biting balm of poetic voice applied to the deep wounds of presidential moral ineptitude and deadly global pandemic."

—ROBERT J. GEORGE
Retired minister, Christian Church (Disciples of Christ)

"... even his prose is poetry..."

—MARCIA CALLIS
Editor, Prophetic Poetry series

*To the dedicated and disappointed resisters
who endured abnormal times during
a racist presidency and a mishandled pandemic.*

*They joined peace protests
to go forward beyond
the degradation of a nation.*

*To the love of my life
Who helped me counteract
this repressive period of time
K*

*To the irrepressible support
of the three amigos
who helped lift this book
out of the dark age of 2017-2021.
Unprecedented Editors:
Kriss Avery
Cheri Avery Black
Jonne Avery Long*

Contents

Introduction	xi
Unprecedented Poem	1
Under Attack	2
Which Way?	3
Trumped Up Sides	4
Fiddling	4
Deconstruction	5
Trumpty Dumpty	7
Handwringing on the Wall	8
The Dump	9
On Destroying a Democracy	10
Innocent Immigrants	11
Voting Again	12
Shutdown	13
Day of Reckoning	14
Questionable Buffer	15
Potholes to Impeachment	16
Sleepwalkers	17
Impeachment Gaps	18
Raise the Bar	19
In the Era of Impeachment	20
Impeachment Obstruction	25
Ignoring Truth	26

Contents

Last Word	27
Parallel Leadership	28
Opposite of Confusion	29
Pants on Fire	30
The Plague	31
Plea for Honesty	32
Mueller Report	33
Beyond Gloom and Doom	34
Ignoring Pandemics and Weapons	35
Corona Fire	36
Uncertainty on a Candidate Trail	37
Transitions	38
Depth Deduction	39
Turned Upside Down	40
Easter Lament	41
Fiasco	42
Masks	43
Invisible Enemy	44
Goo	45
Can Any Good Come From COVID-19?	46
A Different Path	47
A Bout Coronavirus	48
Zip	49
Overwhelming	50
Markings	51
Mental Risk	52
From Bonkers to Benefits	53
Behind the Masks	54
Pivotal	55
Viruses	56
Social Distancing	57

Contents

Complicit	59
Sunset of Discontent	61
Not So Happy Fourth	63
Fright and Flight	64
Stop the Merry-Go-Round	65
Legal Intent	66
Sad Storms	67
Limbo	68
Face Up	69
Poems Instead of Plagues	70
Duped	71
Poem About Trump and COVID-19	72
Crazy Day	73
Hurt in America	74
A New Day	75
Con Games	76
Correcting a Mistake	77
Misplaced	78
What is Wrong with People?	79
What Have We Done to Ourselves?	80
Catatonic	81
Corona Insights	82
Trumptations	83
Hide the Masks (Hypocrisy)	84
Dead End	85
Karma	86
Conspiracy Consumers	87
Fly Bye	88
Headed into the Fall	89
Conundrum	90
Eye on an Election	91

Contents

Protest Vote	92
Biden Says, "Bye Don"	94
A Ghost in the White House	95
Loyalty to a Cult	96
Canyon	97
Democracy In Jeopardy	99
Chasing Hope	100
Momentum in December	101
The Trump Stump	102
Hidden Divide	103
Strands	104
A Christmas Nightmare	106
Insurrection	108
End of an Era	110
Impeached–Again!	112
Postscript: A Beautiful Day	113
Acknowledgements	115
About the Author	117
Books by the Author	119

Introduction

Unprecedented is heard over and over
In reference to an unprecedented President
Whose escapades are first time debacles
Requiring a leap of incredibility over sanity
Putting the nation at risk and ruination

This second stanza of a poem by that name describes the range of President Trump's tenure from 2017—2021 as the "Prez of Chaos." A series of poems capture the unprecedented ruination of a nation and the grief expressed in the despair of living through a low point in a nation's history. Hope was never lost in courageous resistance but it involved waiting for the next election in pursuit of a contentious transfer of power.

These were not normal times. The flaws of a nation were accentuated during the coronavirus pandemic. Hidden divisions wounded civil discourse. Democracy was put at risk. History will not be kind about this era of "making America great again." We will never be the same.

These poems were unprecedented, as well as anything the President ever did. The poems were healthy outlets during the pandemic. Some were uncomfortable. These memorable poems are empathetic partners in helping us go forward.

Unprecedented Poem

A spike in the coronavirus shocks U.S.
And puts a country of anxiety in the lead
With more cases than China or Italy
By exposing flaws in the health system
So we become No. 1 the wrong way

Unprecedented is heard over and over
In reference to an unprecedented President
Whose escapades are first time debacles
Requiring a leap of incredibility over sanity
Putting the nation at risk and ruination

He issued a call to lift the quarantine
So workers could go back on Easter
Around the time when the virus peaks
And the death rate rises from the grave
Which is the opposite of expectations

Unprecedented is the state of the bailout
Which is a nice gesture that doesn't work
So that here we are frustrated and isolated
Staying at home catching up on routines
Or contemplating leisure in avoiding death.

(On occasion when the scare of the coronavirus forces people into their homes to deal with either the noise of their neighbors or the news of impending doom of neighbors faraway)

Under Attack

Trumpism attacks America
    At its core foundation
Destroying democracy
    Dismissing the public good
Relying on selfish greed
    Exaggerating our fears
Using bullying posturing
    To demean our enemies
O for the brave to call for
    Honest communication
"The Emperor has no clothes."

(On occasion of continuing Prophetic Poetry in sending out warnings of a dangerous precedent in American politics)

Which Way?

Low level thinking
Overly concerned about survival
And self-interest at the highest level
Join forces for destruction
When money clouds every vision
And ideologues interfere
With honest pursuit of the truth

Can we save the earth
With enlightenment and vision
Before we blow ourselves up
Or greedily increase global warming?

> *8/4/17 (On occasion of pondering the conundrum: there are forces trying to destroy the earth, but we can join forces that can save the earth by surrounding the earth with enlightenment and a vision of peace)*

Trumped Up Sides

Fascism visited Charlottesville
    Spewing out violence
        Which passed the amoral test
Of a President who defended
The equal rights of both sides
    To express themselves
        When hate and racism are repugnant.

Fiddling

The Prez tweeted;
    Rome burned.

(On occasion when this started by what we said, "The Prez will take this country down," but to actually see it with the help of the virus—Sad)

Deconstruction

So quick to destroy
What takes so long
To build up
    Like a two-year old
    Knocking down blocks
    Just to hear them crash
So goes the White House
    These days of deconstruction
        That take away
            The non-profits
                Of concern for the poor
In favor of a business operation
    That makes money for the rich
        By piling money into the military
            And ignoring, even assaulting
                the welfare of the people
And if this was the agenda
    Of the conservatives
    How do they live with themselves
        Knowing that it looks selfish
            Even sneaky and dishonest
                To out-maneuver the resistance
                By avoiding questions
                    That disclose the truth
The divisions are painful
    The ethics of the greater good
        Are lost in superficiality
The forces of fear push away
    The gentler persuasion of love
        So it seems so it seems

Violence doesn't always prevail
Enough people can turn about
    The destruction of the climate
        Or save a nation from ruination
    But this is our hope, a fragile hope
        Like a last-second basketball shot
    So close but it's not just one game
We are still given another chance
  If we are spared from the nuclear option
As the Good Book reminds us
  To choose life over death
  As long as we breathe our next breath.

(On occasion in which the dismantling of a nation has surreptitiously occurred)

Trumpty Dumpty

Tearing up a society
    Seems impossible
        But wrenching children
            From sobbing mothers
                Is unconscionable
Such cases unfold in real time
    To the astonishment of gatherers
        Of the Poor People Campaign
Who are asking, "How low?"
    Will the morals go
        With the trail of tough talk—
            Always leaving abuses
                And hurt feelings
So Trumpty Dumpty needs
    To be put back together again
        By reordering a new set of values
            Or starting over
We may wait for a big fall,
    But we will pick up the pieces
        And work for Peace again.

(On occasion when the Poor People's Campaign covered Washington DC on June 23, 2018)

Handwringing on the Wall

Unconscionable when all
    Trump wants for Christmas
    Is a WALL, a billion dollar
    Imprisonment to shut out
    Both sides from each other
Dirty and divided indifference
    A front line war zone of cruelty
    Showing the worst of selfishness
    Separating children forever ignored
    That is the way it is—so what?
    News goes to the next distraction
We are drugging our populace
    To withstand the excruciating pain
    To detach every person from reality
    So we lose all empathy for humanity
May Christmas tear down our own walls
    For the handwriting is on the wall
    We can no longer vote destruction
    Into power and survive another birth.

(On occasion of wondering how some people voted for destructive leadership during each cycle of Christmas to ask if we will build walls or give birth to a new humanity)

The Dump

Trump hits a speed bump
Slowing funds for the wall
No more will Demos jump
After his mojo joins the fall.

*1/26/19 (On occasion of resistance after 35 days
when the government shut down ends)*

On Destroying a Democracy

How much mean can you stand
    Before you change policy or party
Whereas the law trumps compassion
    By ripping babies from mother's breasts
And locking youth in cages
    Making mean-spirited seem normal?

The cruelty to humans suffers children
    To lose their innocence to early death
Until we have done irreparable harm
    And cause tenderness to disappear
And turn into brutish stubborn bullies
    Who have lost the ability to empathize.

What does it take to see another way
    To raise our children with choices
And question the military use of force?
    The artistic spark needs freedom
To provide a nurturing atmosphere
    More than just rules and regulations.

*(On occasion of hearing how immigrants are
separated inhumanely into detention centers)*

Innocent Immigrants

The ground of being Peace
    Emerges out of the divide

Even though the forces of evil
    Push away innocent children

And fail to recognize that we
    Are the cause of immigration

When we create the cartels
    That cause the drug violence

Wake us up to own the problem
    And protect innocent children.

7/9/18 (On occasion of realizing that the cartels, made up of drug thugs, push immigrants to our border, according to Jennifer Harber, well-known Immigration Attorney)

Voting Again

I still mourn
    The same feelings
        I felt in the shock
            of Nov. 5th 2016
            When I felt
Our soul was jerked from us
    And we could project
        The pain slicing my gut
            Into minutia pieces
And we could look back
    At the dismantling of America
        And the eroding of democracy
            And the violent use of force
Vulnerable,
    I gathered myself
        Gave time later to heal my soul
            And voted on a new beginning.

10/29/18 (On occasion of knowing that leadership does make a difference but sometimes we need to wait it out)

Shutdown

What was historic
    About this diverse Congress
        Was an energizing of politics
            On January 3, 2019
When the move
    To reopen government
        Made an end run
            Around the wall
And demonstrated
    Where the negativity
        And paralysis resides
            In a bunch of GOPers
Who shut the door
    And slammed their noses
        In the crack because
            It was long like Pinocchio's.

1/4/19 (On occasion when Nancy Pelosi added a spark by stepping up to be Speaker of the House and actually said something that made sense, i.e., to reopen)

Day of Reckoning

The tide is changing
The night is turning to day
When the season of winter
    Gives way to spring
        Fresh and honest
The testimony was painful
    As a loyal cover-upper
        Turned evidence
            Of wrong doing
Over the months of agony
    When lies piled on lies
        And values trampled
            On the pure and good
Suddenly a bold, bigger bang
    Of light sprinkled shadows
        Of peace across the span
            Over decades of divide.

2/28/19 (On occasion of February 27, 2019 when the testimony of Michael Cohen finally set straight much of the lies of the highest office in the land)

Questionable Buffer

The Prez has stirred the nest
    And the wasps are buzzing
        Around his impeachment

Because he meddled in dirt
    And withheld military aid
        And betrayed an ally

Woe are the times we stumble
    And do the opposite
        Of what is expected of US

For it may just be that Donald
    Avoided war and loss of life
        By conceding a buffer zone

A complicated mishmash
    Of sticking it to the Kurds
        And favoring all the turkeys

So now we have realignments
    And future uncertainties even
        A tenuous no peace zone.

        9/18/19 (On occasion of seeing a rough week of impeachment possibilities and failure to keep commitments with an ally)

Potholes to Impeachment

The Prez sees no wrongdoing
Neither do his followers

Even the blizzard of scandal
Recognizes the ruin-nation

Sad are days of impeachment
When no one is above the law

Some religion pretends that God
Will save them from consequences

But the cold eye of history will not
Forget this travesty of misgivings

The road will have many potholes
To avoid driving this way again.

9/24/19 (On occasion when House Speaker Nancy Pelosi announced a formal inquiry for impeachment of Donald Trump)

Sleepwalkers

Scared—about elections
Who wouldn't be?

Nixon voted in
A second time
Before resigning

Bush voted in
A second time
After we knew
About a trumped up war

Then there is Trump
Living in a fantasy world
Blaming Ukraine
For Russian interference
Yet people worship him

Have they fallen off a cliff
And bumped their heads?
The NFL would sideline
Concussions. Can we?
Do the same
Before playing "citizen."

> *11/22/19 (On occasion after Intel Committee finished off impeachment hearings when witnesses to the truth confront conspiracy theories, as if denial and deception loves hypocrisy)*

Impeachment Gaps

The divide between two perspectives
    Seems to be more vertical than horizontal
Moving farther apart from gaps side by side
    Into walls of alienation and polarities
While the real distinction comes from a column
    Up and down, with the same base
Except the glass half full represents values
    That are concerned for survival needs
And higher ideals float to the top
    Reaching skyward into authenticity needs
Much like the pyramid icon of Maslow
    Layered on top of lower needs
Which are based on self-preservation,
    Tangible and practical and sensorial
Rather than intuitive and abstract and idealistic
    Interlocked yet worlds apart are two ways
That are suspicious of one another,
    The lower wants to fight and stop change
    The higher wants to raise the social spirit
Two mixed perspectives claim to be better,
    One feels comfortable seeing the mud
    And the other looks toward the stars.

12/18/19 (On an historic day in which Trump is impeached and receives attention he requires, if only we can spare the destruction)

Raise the Bar

Impeachment arrives
In the solemn walk to the Senate
Bringing anger on both sides
As the Great Divider and
Media Manipulation
Numb the ability to think.

Down we go
    Nice guys and all
    Tightening their blindfolds
    Pushing on their headsets
    Remaining silent to the poor
    Ignoring nuclear games

Spare us from demise
Reduce the rhetoric
Allow for a higher honesty
Raise the bar.

1/15/20 (On occasion when proceedings began in a sacred parade of managers in carrying articles of impeachment to the Senate and the swearing in of jurors the next day by Chief Judge John Roberts of the Supreme Court)

In the Era of Impeachment

Impeachment requires silence
    On pain of imprisonment
As Senators are quarantined
    Behind desks in the chamber
A solemn and serious imposition
    To listen to the evidence
To determine any breaking of law

Checks and balances were at stake
    In reining in a rogue President
Who pushes on every boundary
    To create a defiant aberration
That challenges normal procedure

Sergeant of arms introduced
    Seven managers to enact the trial
On President Donald John Trump
    To wake from stonewalling truth
Of abuse of power and obstruction

Senators were sworn in by signing
    Their names in an oath book stating
Articles of impeachment in a rare moment
    When all the senators were present

Senators are supposed to listen
    Without the use of digital devices
Difficult in an age of hyperactivity
    Yet the data was already available

First there was the personal lawyer
    Michael Cohen in the first chapter
Then came Ukrainian Lev Parnas
    Of the second chapter of transparency
Both scorned for pushing a hoax

But the case propelled solemnly
    Under Chief Justice John Roberts
Revealing a trove of documents
    Contradicting the President's reality
Questions came up about a fair trial
    By denial of documents and witnesses
Trying to break the cover up in the loop
    To hear relevant voices hiding the truth

Such as witness Mulvaney commenting
    On the hold back of money to Ukraine
Minimizing the withholding of aid,
    "I have news for you; get over it!"

House managers put out the evidence
    Such as from Hakeem Jeffries so that
McConnell asked to stack amendments
    Necessary for following the timeline

Rep Adam Schiff seemed touched
    By his own words during the opening
When he revealed Mulvaney's boast
    That we need to get over it, no big deal
As he conjectured a national decline
    Asserting that impeachment was urgent

Ukraine Ambassador Marie Yovanovitch
    According to Jerry Nadler was confused
Why she was abruptly called home
    A sudden casualty of a smear campaign
Which resulted in deteriorating conditions
    Noting that lies chase fictional information

Holding funds from Ukraine was intentional
    In forcing an announcement about corruption
And linking it to a political rival—the Bidens
    For personal advantage in the next election
The scheme kept producing corroboration
    Which was an incredible amount of energy
Put into redacted documents on the cover up

The challenge is how far this scheme spreads
    As Rep. Schiff details the convoluted scheme
Where on July 25 a perfect call unloads chaos
    Springing an aftermath of power and obstruction

Alexander Vindman confirmed his duty
    That right matters in the face of corruption
Because the Diplomatic Corp served the nation
    Not captured by personal domestic politics
Sylvia Garcia underlined the abuse of power
    Reminding Senators of the depth of wrongs

The confusing evidence from the House managers
    Seemed incomplete until John Bolton's bombshell
Surfaced from his manuscript of a link between
    Direct ties of withholding aid and finding Biden dirt
Which opens up the need to hear more witnesses
    Even after the defense used red herrings to claim
That there was not enough impeachable evidence

Constitutional lawyer Alan Dershowitz showed up
    To require criminal behavior to the level of treason
Rather than lesser abuse and obstruction of Congress
    He offers a view to deal with conflicts: the shoe test:
Step into the other shoe, rather than a better shoe

The Defense never rose to a level of moral courage
    Refusing to call witnesses, preferring a quick trial
Kicking the can of truth down the road of confusion
    Sticking heads in the sand and hiding in their tribe

Yikes! Wow! The Bolton surprise
    Became a central figure of conjecture
In offering a flurry of unresolved interest
    By extending the curiosity for testimony

The volcano of eruption focuses
    Smoke on a firestorm of scandal
When Trump removed an ambassador
    Illegally so alluded to by Sen. Engel
As the trial moved into Senator questions

In response to questions about witnesses
    Trials require witnesses and documents
To render a verdict that needs facts
    But the concern was a tie up in courts
When other times it was revealed quickly

The fear is an autocratic President
    Capable of doing anything he wants
Without responsibility to a democracy
    Making the President above the law

House managers pleaded for witnesses
    To search for the truth in a fair trial
But leaks keep coming about John Bolton
    Who offers a narration filling in the gaps

Late Friday afternoon tears saddened hearts
    As the vote to deny witnesses tallied its 51
Bringing a darkness to truth while most
    Returned home without a pall of regret

Joining the wrong doing of a President
    Who is free of consequences yet marked
By impeachment, a sham trial, sordid values
    As truth is subjected to a national disgrace.

So Senators leave to watch the Super Bowl
    But was there more at stake than another game
Where one can be selfish and get away with it
    By shivering into a knot of majority lies? When?
Will America rise up again for moral courage?

> *1/31/20 (On occasion when the majority of Senators went home to take in the simpler conflict of Chiefs over 49ers after a grueling fight on Impeachment)*

Impeachment Obstruction

Incredible when
Undermining institutions
By President of USA
Finally reached a coup
For Russia to take advantage
By manipulating our elections
Showing Putin standing
Side by side flouting propaganda
About investigating Biden
The same pattern of interfering
With the theory of losing
Thirty thousand Emails

Adam Schiff stepped into the shoes
Of Marie Yovanovitch losing her job
Or anyone who blocked the President's schemes
Using his power to cheat for
Personal gain, this will not stop
Questioning what really matters
About which false conspiracies count

Sounding the alarm, repeatedly
The danger of foreign influence persists
That we can not get over it
So this character of leadership
Will continue to advance his goals
And diminish the country's interest
Asserting "He must be removed."

1/23/20 (On occasion when the President was not removed and we moved into the campaign season to replace him)

Ignoring Truth

Some believe truth is overrated
Since some prefer . . . Ignorance
   It is blissful
       Less tiring
       In the realm of dreaming innocence
So truth is ignored, too hard,
   Or will it set us free
       With an illuminated mindset
          In the trial?
Too often,
   Ignorance trumps truth.

(On occasion of listening to the Senate questions examining the truth of the President and his cult of followers)

Last Word

Nancy Pelosi shredded the text
    Of the State of the Union speech
    Plagiarized by President Trump
As if he were mouthing sentimental
    Trivia at a pedantic funeral elegy
    Totally full of sham falsehoods
Hyperbole oozed from the display
    Of hypocrisy in shameful view
    As lies disgraced the occasion
Trumpeted by head bobbing GOPers
    Applauding all exceptionalism
    Even chanting, "Four more years."

Then when he used the occasion
    To bestow the Medal of Freedom
    Upon radio host Rush Limbaugh
The right wing theatre was exposed
    As a pompous reality show charade

Once again a certain level of mindset
    Only sees the lowest sensual instincts
Rather than higher levels of authenticity
    Requiring respect for spiritual values,
Discernable through critical thinking
    By civility and honesty setting us free.

    (On occasion of listening to a State of the Union speech by President
        Trump during the dark days of impeachment and division)

Parallel Leadership

When Germany tasted toxic elements
    With the leadership of Hitler
        And ovens blazed into a Holocaust
            That turned humanity vicious
So it makes one wonder if the end
    Came from the dropping of a bomb
        Or the removal of white nationalism
            From the persuasive grip of Nazism
The scary arrival of Trump 71 years later
    Shows parallels to containment cages
        And a culture of unprecedented violence
            All devoted to right wing extremism
The persuasion of leadership unleashes
    Powerful forces that can turn destructive
        Or bring about good honest civil discourse
            Free of racism and working for progress.

8/7/19 (On occasion when the link to autocracy and white supremacy is too familiar, even though the style of leadership is not the same)

Opposite of Confusion

The right of Transgenders
   To decide their identity
      Seems tolerantly different
         And acceptable to others
Looking at opposites requires
   Discovering the starting point
      By settling on the norm
         Of what is the status quo
Conservatives set the standard
   Controlling the popular rules
      Which liberals find abhorrent
         Unless you want Trumpism
Which leads to a kind of chaos
   Where the norms are valueless
      Opposite of higher ideals
         Where racism loses out
Thus Transgenders, immigrants
   Those who are different
      Are shut out of a democracy
         That allows equality for all.
How will we end up going down
   When those who voted blindly
      For Donald Trump get walls
         While the rest of us suffer?

10/13/19 (On occasion of hearing a CBS report on a "trans" part of the equation of LGBTQ alphabet variety and how a Trump world finds lies by excluding these communities)

Pants on Fire

Just the sound of Trump
    Makes me recoil in shock
        At the thought of terror
When everything in me
    Screams like a siren,
        "Beware of the fire!"
And the trumpet answers,
    "He is wonderful and
        Done all he promised."
And that's what's frightening,
    That people will say that,
        And follow him into limbo
Nah! This is only a disillusion
    And the pendulum will swing
        To make corrections.
Maybe! Perhaps Not. Scary, Huh.
    We are in a downward spiral
        Fighting burning rain forests
Wiping out the lungs of the earth
    Choking out, "We can't breathe,"
        Gasping for another news cycle.

2019 (On occasion in hearing a Trump supporter and outlasting the lies)

The Plague

The creepy crawl of COVID-19
Snatches up victims like snacks
Spreading paralytic parasites
Into pandemic corners of the world

This plague of fear pounces quickly
On the least of the unsuspecting
And shuts down all sports activity
Even gatherings of entertainment

Whatever happened to rock and roll
When we find more rock than roll
And are stuck alone and scared
Asking if we might roll differently.

> *3/15/20 (On occasion when the world was hit by a pandemic and fear stopped "March Madness" for a different kind of choice, not always the better)*

Plea for Honesty

    Bizarre idea
    Sensationalism
A spoof on intelligence

    What would cause a snake-oil salesman
To promote the injection of disinfectant
    Into the body of a COVID-19 victim?
What is the propensity of the right wing
    To follow the nonsense of Trumpism?
Many are scratching their heads in disbelief
    That party loyalists would fall off a cliff
        Shamelessly for this Prez of Chaos
            Who has dismantled a wounded nation
Besieged by militia groups
    Attacked by racist rhetoric
        Defended by a blind political ignorance
            Afraid of including others different

There seems to be a lack of honesty
    Maybe that's it, dishonesty
        To examine the adequacy of positions
To listen in understanding the other side
    To concede a little for the good of dialogue
        To forgive ourselves for our foolishness
            To trade out some of our principles
                To be less defensive of our fragile pride

The division is hurting the soul of our nation,
    And will continue long after COVID-19 leaves
        Unless we use our minds to accept others
            With enough love to quit punishing each other.

                4/24/20 (On occasion to make an honest reply beyond
                name-calling about a proposal to deal with the coronavirus
                but also to throw out an olive branch for civil discourse)

Mueller Report

The lies pull us into quicksand
    Sucking us into the awful mire
        Possibly lawful but awful
So awful that truth turns murky
    Yet it comes out persistently,
        Agitating like a barking dog.

                (The delay was exasperating by its own conservative spin on
                April 18. 2019 but the Mueller Report delivered a tour de force
                to the Prez of Chaos, who continued to bark at it)

Beyond Gloom and Doom

Friday the Thirteenth
    Came and went
Noting the advancement
    Of impeachment
        For the Prez of Chaos
And the demise of the GOP
    Morphed into the image
        Of Donald Trump
Plus the strong-arm push
    For Brexit and Boris
        In a breakup move
        On the United Kingdom
We move into the New Year
    Singing, "Merry Christmas
    Gloom and Doom all around,
    People dying everywhere,"
But then we hear faint echoes
    Of Peace on earth, and
    Joy to the world . . . obviously,
A momentary indulgence –
    Like encouragement to go on.

        12/13/19 (On occasion to find the holy in Happy Holidays)

Ignoring Pandemics and Weapons

The coronavirus set off alarms globally
Yet end of the world warnings are ignored
When it comes to highly triggered bombs
That could go nuclear a thousand times
The radioactive devastation of Hiroshima

Organized activities summarily ceased
Stocks plummeted, sports halted play
Times Square became a ghost town
As people stayed home feeling isolated
And stunned by the rapid leap of deaths

And deceived by diversions of a President
Impeachable, unreachable, irresponsible
Trying to dismiss the gravity of a pandemic
By delaying preparation to stem its impact
Since he miscalculated it as a case of the flu

Obviously it is more serious than the flu
Like dismissing the threat of nuclear weapons
As the final chapter of eliminating humanity
But we would have to be as scared as a pandemic
To sanely remove the missiles that could harm us.

(On occasion when seventeen protestors were given trespassing charges on Nov. 1, 2020 in Kansas City by ignoring their urgent message of global annihilation but by contrast COVID-19 received obedient compliance)

Corona Fire

A distant fire truck screams an alarm
That a fire is spreading out of control
As fast as the Corona firewater comes virus 19
Exponentially consuming first victims

Everyone is first in this new era of germs
That has maliciously attacked humanity
Frightened and hiding from this mass killer
With no known answer to its evil rampage

Dr. Lee of Wuhan China was the first
To recognized that something was wrong
And warned that a pandemic was imminent
But his alarm was silenced and he died

Officials in denial did not adequately prepare
For this tenacious predator shutting nations down
Nor did they offer much hope for the dying
Sequestered and counted as anonymous statistics

About a century after the Great Depression of 1929
History will now record its Dark Devastation of 2020
And people will remember the stock market crash
When a quarantined world was brought to its knees
Praying that at least it wasn't as final as a nuclear war.

*(On occasion in hoping for a chance to live through
the devastation of March 2020)*

Uncertainty on a Candidate Trail

Instability
The corona is a feared virus
That spreads like wildfire water
Making drinkers deliriously drunk
In a self induced coma
To binge obnoxiously trancelike
And seek safety in numbers.

Uncertainty
Living through a Trump era
Which challenges familiarity
To normal expectations
And threatens societal sanity
Reducing the dignity of a nation

No wonder Dem candidates fold
Joining the Biden team
To avoid the sheer craziness
That disrupts lackadaisical times
Trying to slow the fear
Of a Bernie train wreck
Which rides a destiny of progress
And has the energy to capture
The imagination of a new future.

3/5/20 (On occasion of a pull back on Bernie Sanders'
new deal of socialism to care for people)

Transitions

Previous winter has shut down the outside
    Trees bare their leaves of lonely limbs
    Fracturing the grey sky in stark lines
    Shivering in cold unprotected desperation

For the warm light of a budding springtime
    Where green pops out from wooden warts
    And ants scurry free from hibernation
    And birds join the dance of mating rituals

Thrusting the winter of COVID-19 into Spring
    When the debate of candidates Joe and Bernie
    Contrasts a slow evolution with a revolution
    To expand or do over the health care system
    To fine tune ecology or tackle climate change

To play it safe or introduce a different approach
    During a time when a horrific disease disrupts
    Normal routines, social outlets and stability
    In democratic functions and health concerns

What will result in a Trump or COVID-19 siege?
    Do we have a chance for a new transition?
    Questions surround doubts about how to live
    In Seasons opting for fear or care, maybe both.

                    3/17/20 (On occasion when tumultuous waves
                            of change threaten our survival and health)

Depth Deduction

In the period of the Trump dump
    When he dropped the Paris Agreement
    The Climate became dangerously tearful
As an Empire lost its ability to care
    Feeling isolated and unloved
    Without a moral compass, only greed
    By taking advantage of others
Yet some baby steps began to move forward
    When youth led the March of our Lives
    Through the false security of guns
And the Poor People's Campaign opened eyes
    To be sensitive to the vulnerable
    And use policy to care for the least of these
We are on a sad journey if we lose substance
    And settle for entertainment glitter
    And fail to contribute coronavirus mulch foundation.

(Upon occasion in coming to Good Friday and thinking of all the crucifixions in which we hurt others)

Turned Upside Down

An inner sadness fills Good Friday
When the wave of the coronavirus
Sweeps across an ill-equipped nation
Unprepared for its lethal assault
Already having raced toward the abyss
Under the countdown of 100 seconds
Before the doomsday clock drops
The Capitol curtain on a Freak Show
Cast by a sociopath and clueless actors
In an echo chamber behind his directives
Spewing tortured words of a mad man
Destined for a Shakespearian tragedy
Which feels like a nation under crucifixion

If there is an Easter hope rising anywhere
Then we will have escaped the pandemic
But also we will see hope in small groups
Of young and old people all around us
Who take on values of peace and justice
Invoking courageous actions of non-violence
By turning up side down lower expectations
To adopt higher signs of the Eastertide season.

(On occasion of living through an Easter week of spiked pandemics when we are staying at home on Good Friday to wonder about abnormal behavior)

Easter Lament

Easter week turns a corner
As it does in its annual fanfare
Pulsating a dynamic rhythm
Of crucifixion and resurrection
But mostly a week of loss
Of loved lives and endless wars

But this time COVID-19 appeared
With a vengeance as a vicious virus
That shut a frightened world down
And in many places reaching an apex
Of death, destruction, and desperation

Hiding in homes or on the front lines
Where hospitals were overwhelmed
By ill-equipped health care workers
Fighting for victims to their final breath
And in many cases pained by the inevitable

This was a 911 and Holocaust moment
That marked nations for crucifixion
No longer talking about war on each other

But how to share the lament in their silences
Which brought home an historic Easter
    To accept vulnerability pushing us off-schedule
    To dig deeper than artificial appearances
    To rise to the endurance of the human spirit.

> *4/6/20 (On occasion when the 2020 pandemic took control of our interrupted lives at the highest count of deaths, certainly more than current wars but far short of a total nuclear annihilation)*

Fiasco

COVID-19 exposed inadequacies
    To protect our survival
We risk a fiasco in
    Bloated military budgets
    Medicare for All
    Green New Deal responses

Let's cut the military by half
    Redirect budget to Medicare for All
    And to an ecology of climate change
    By eliminating nuclear weapons
        Threatening total destruction
        And failing to support our planet

PeaceWorks belongs to a movement
    That brings awareness to the fiasco
    Of the new nuclear plant
    And the preemptive strikes
    Of Hiroshima and Nagasaki
    That we need to change to survive
    Lest we forget our own peril.

4/14/20 (On occasion of enduring the virus and seeing the need to audit and reduce military spending, redirecting adequate support for health care and a Green New Deal)

Masks

The virus has made faceless masses
Too numerable to hide one's identity

Humanity joins the anonymity of death
Becoming a statistic of the grand plague

No one can ride into a spectacular sunset
Known like the Lone Ranger behind a mask

All are insignificant like ants marching on
Two by two wearing our invisible masks

We play a role in the human enterprise
Becoming significant by being vulnerable

When we reach out to another long distant
We take off our masks to relate authentically.

> 4/2/20 (On occasion during the coronavirus crisis when so many are talking about masks, not endless war, but a phone call makes one realize that we are not alone in facing this ordeal)

Invisible Enemy

Sneak attack
    This coronavirus
    Leaving mayhem behind
Didn't see it coming
    The plague of locusts
    Eating up Africa
Passwords that don't work
    Frustrating computer work
Netflix becoming overloaded
    Denying any relief
The danger of uranium
    Hiding behind nuclear weapons
So much of our lives
    Are shaped by invisible enemies
Vulnerable, we don't even know
    When we will die
Because we can't remember
    A newly assigned password
Some days just seem unfair!
    So we say "It could be worse"
    Saved by the grace of intimacy.

4/15/20 (On occasion of listening to TV about a spike in the deaths from the coronavirus, added pain from locusts, and computer problems. We need to find more healthy ways to cope in dining at home)

Goo

Goo . . . melting . . . oozing
    Off the President's lips
    Dripping into a pooh
    of germy BS–like muck

The syrupy drip of boasts
    Exaggerates the false hype
    Of a nation's greatness
    Fleeing from the coronavirus
    Yet statistics signify nothing
    Except dishonest babbling
    In phony hushed tones

That is what is most disturbing—
    The lies that cover the inactions
    And somehow seem hollow
    Steering away from the truth—
    Better death than hypocrisy.

4/17/20 (On occasion of questioning a White House briefing and seeing enough chaos to write this poem)

Can Any Good Come From COVID-19?

The common enemy is COVID-19
    For both the Far-right and Liberals
But the fight plays out between the two
    Creating artificial lines of division
Pitting a Far-right cry for America first
    Backed up by the Second Amendment
Against a plea for rational fact-based
    Orders to isolate the spreading virus
One side wants to return to work as usual
    While the other accepts an unusual break

So here we have it—conflicting desires
    For familiar routines of economic gain
    Or time out to explore a new reality

Caught in the tension of work and leisure
    Between survival and higher values
    Between eating out and intimate dining in
    Between fear and love of new projects
    Between paying bills and reading a book
    Between following orders and thinking time
    Between national security and helping the poor
    Between using force and non-violent action
    Between love of things and love of family
Whatever, COVID-19 gives US sobering choices.

4/20/20 (On occasion when deaths have doubled in a week and the push from the right is to return to the way things used to be)

A Different Path

COVID-19 came along to shock us
   Out of any false pretenses
   That we live in a perfect, plastic
      Wonderful world
I guess I don't fit in crowds
   That spread their sickening virus
   By masquerading a false image
      Of how amazingly popular they are
I find that I'm on the trail
   That took a different path
      a seeker of truth
         one who avoids rule makers
            a listener wrapped in calming music
               a gazer feeling the hug of nature
        a lover of the squeeze of my beloved
          a pursuer of an ultimate concern for Peace
         a raging protester against injustice
            one who doesn't like others to destroy trees
            one who is vulnerable, insignificant, and almost nothing
   So I meet this day, knowing that I'm not alone
But traveling into an unknown virus
   With loving companions, who may know or not
      I like being suspiciously authentic.

                4/23/20 (On occasion of facing an unknown virus
                            and not knowing if I'm half crazy)

A Bout Coronavirus

Today was going to open up shops
    After stay-at-home orders lifted
But rational people questioned this
    After a million plus cases and
    Sixty thousand deaths surged numbers
Monday blues arrive with torrential rains
    Crying big tears over the delusions
    Of lost employment and disrupted plans
What hurt most was our inability to smile
    Hidden behind our masks and pretenses
    Pumping up charades of cheerfulness
    When all we really feel is home alone
Someday we will renew friendships
    And sonorous enticements of conversation
    But meanwhile we accept our invisibility
    Having lost the passwords to our hearts
For the compassionate way to stay connected
    Is to navigate in an era of electronic dismay
    By solving the secrets of our passwords
    And absorbing the frustration of rejection
Now is the time to accept social distancing
    Finding doses of love in the winds of change
    By avoiding any contagious dance partners.

5/4/20 (On occasion when more than endurance and luck is needed to avoid an acute bout with COVID-19)

Zip

The coronavirus removes the "zip"
    From the mental health of America
    Led by the behavior of its leader
    Who defies the advice of scientists
COVID-19 sneaks around in dark places
    Attaching its grip on innocent victims
    Who have lowered their resistance
    To quietly bolster their immune systems
As is the seduction of far-right ideology
    Taking the entrapment of the easy way
    By worrying about survival more than
    Expanding the goals of authentic living
    By embracing mind, body and spirit
    To challenge the limits of one's potential
Instead of how low we can go to survive
    We need energy to break out of quarantines
    Of selfishness and fear of the next step
    Finding courage for peace and justice issues
What matters most in life in the long view
    That puts "zip" in a planet without harming it.

5/6/20 (On occasion when mourning news requires something good to counterbalance its devastation)

Overwhelming

Overwhelming—
    A word without limits
    But a feeling of distress
    When lost beyond the limits

Sounding like unemployment
    Waking up to the 14.7% jobless
    Which doesn't begin to handle
    The anguish of bills to juggle
    And the fear of disappearing
    Under a pile of dropped balls

Like more rain in the forecast
    Flooding the basement of COVID-19
    Reporting despair in cases and deaths
    Leaving one numb and scary dumb
    Hiding behind anonymous masks

If we can live through this historic era
    May we stop the cacophony of stress
    Pausing to breathe and look around
    At waving leaves blowing in the wind
    Praying into a larger wonder of life
    Hearing the calm of favorite music
    Resting in the arms of our beloved
    Finding humor in the simplest joys
    Taking on projects that build things
    Dining on meals that taste erotic
    Discerning politics that make sense

So wash hands, breathing 20 seconds
    of hope.

*5/8/20 (On occasion in hearing rising figures
of unemployment and coronavirus deaths)*

Markings

During this coronavirus
One wonders
About the vertigo of time
When one used to know
Which day of the week it was
By routine events to pick up groceries
When to go to a favorite restaurant
When to go to the hairdresser
What day to go to church

Now one lives in virtual reality
Timeless and adrift
Absorbed in a good book
Scanning the Internet
Going for a walk in nature
And if fortunate enough
Living in perpetual retirement
Letting some things go
And finding new projects
Loving to be, sometimes not to do
Looking for markings of the spirit.

*(On occasion in shifting tracks to more leisurely
pursuits while staying free of COVID-19)*

Mental Risk

A double whammy comes from COVID-19
    One involving cases of virus and death
    Yet toll on mental stress is debilitating

Ensnarling the feeling of forced isolation
    Like persons quarantined in prison
    Missing the vitality of social interaction
    And in many cases suffering from hunger
    And deprivation of mental stimulation
    Triggering low self–esteem and addiction

An invisible plague creeps into paralysis
    So that one is afraid to care any longer
    Joining statistics of surrendering casualties

Unless one cares enough to confront the risks
    If one could be so lucky to avoid one statistic
    By wearing masks and keeping a distance
    And discovering loving spaces at home.

5/15/20 (On occasion when the okay was given to cut hair but not okay to dine at restaurants, since the statistics have not yet flattened the risks of the virus)

From Bonkers to Benefits

COVID-19 exposes the vulnerability of America
    By demanding a return to work from the top
    And failing to provide protection from the virus
    Reaching the worst statistic for cases and deaths
    Piling skewed outrage on top of skewed outrage
    While silencing the critics of a flawed system

But we do live through contradictory shadows
    And can find pockets of creativity in hidden places

During this pandemic we found projects to build
    We expanded our ideas in good solid books
    We relished our privacy free of appointments
    Some dirtied hands in gardens of nature's delight
    Others calmed themselves in the music of the soul
    We dined on meals enhancing our culinary tastes
    We jived and played in intimate relationships
    We joked and laughed over the political landscape

Turns out that social distancing was a benefit
    Not only from the virus but from the harsher sides
        That deny scientific support
        That are fascinated by conspiracy theories
        That assign mean attacks on excluded groups
        That outline budgets for heavy military solutions

Maybe someday civil discussion will unite us.

5/20/20 (On occasion when stay-at-home preventions from the coronavirus were eased during a time that governance was out of control)

Behind the Masks

Indulgent praise echoes flat
    In the chambers of public noise
        When the cries for help are muted

Rejecting a mask is a defiant statement
    In the face of 100,000 COVID-19 deaths
        That says I am foolish or I don't care

The President rejects its political correctness
    As a fashion statement against the virus
        That he can look good and be a renegade

And somehow the masks are tied into racism
    Where superiority tosses caution to the wind
        And too many people of color are infected

This leader boosts his ego by suspending reality
    Yet he fails to mention any lack of response
        That promoted a surge in corona casualties

How low can we go and still be called Great?
    Some predicted that he could ruin the country
        We have arrived—shamed, numbed, and weary
        Waiting behind our masks on an election.

        5/27/20 (On occasion of an historic day when 100,000 deaths from the coronavirus surpassed any loss from wars)

Pivotal

The soft flutter of leaves in the trees belie
    The waves of restlessness in a nation
    As protests lap the shoreline of racism
    And quickly disperse in the sands of history
No one might notice that the tough Trump
    Retreats to a bunker, fires a whistleblower
    Orders pepper spray on a protest crowd
    Camouflages behind a Bible, irreverently
    Positions the military at the Lincoln Memorial
    Threatens to place military guards on the streets
    Agitates the worst values behind the hypocrisy
Truly reminiscent of Nazi behavior in dictators
    Completely dismissing Constitutional protocol
    Rampaging a fear campaign on national freedom
    Approving a George Floyd-like repression
        On a nation's ability to breathe and live again
Yes this is a pivotal moment to lose our democracy
    Or to gain energy to find the conscience of America
    Whether we find roots in legalism or good choices
    Whether we will promote destruction or creation.

        6/4/20 (On occasion during the ninth day of emotional protests
            when the doors of a nation have come unhinged)

Viruses

America has two viruses out of control
    Four months of COVID-19 and
    Four hundred years of racism
Both of which are missing a quick vaccine
    As both have resorted to social distancing
    Except that racism has endured force
    By white bullies enforcing the status quo
    Through systemic violence and intolerance
The fear of both has plagued a mental obsession
    So that one is distracted from real solutions
    Toward climate change and nuclear weapons
    Safe to say, "Start by putting away the guns,"
    Possessed to dominate by fearful distancing
Learn to get along gently and communicate
    On higher goals beyond the cultural divide
    As to racism let us "wash our hands"
    And shift to focus on primary issues of survival.

6/5/20 (On occasion during the tenth protest on the incident of George Floyd to ask if one can move from racism to other core issues of survival)

Social Distancing

Lifelines are cut off
During the coronavirus
In which jobs are lost
And income dissipates
Forcing homelessness
And fear of depression
Out in lonely soup lines

Transfixed by their phones
People were already lonely
But not anxious like this
Worried about getting close
By breathing the death germ

They had nothing to expect
In the way of entertainment
And fun activities with friends
They were isolated ready to die
Six feet distant in the ground

Not everyone felt this way
Some went on spring breaks
Others flew down ski slopes
Many defied unlucky casualties
Looking death straight in the eye

They ran the obstacle course
Bragging they were an exception
But some were humbly contrite
Realizing they interconnected
With the hurt and joy of humanity.

3/18/20 (On occasion when the rising death toll from COVID-19 slowed down human interaction and loneliness provided a checklist of one's priorities)

Complicit

I mourn the time our nation lost its way
    When an election turned a nation to ruin-nation
    As all the signs of demolition were obvious
    To a thinking person who had political savvy
    Except I hid my anger toward brazen friends
    Who had the audacity to vote him in
        Free of consequences and unapologetic
        Thus ignorant of his risk to democracy

I could not share the words of my pain
    To watch the dismantling of Obama's legacy
    To see how bullies use force to abuse others
    To stand by while immigrant families are torn apart
    To listen to language that dehumanizes people
    To feel the atmosphere of fear creep over the land
    To build walls as symbols of division and exclusion
    To experience the breakdown of trust in diplomacy
    To drop international cooperation like WHO
    To stare at the hypocrisy in hiding behind a Bible
    To sense helplessness in the onset of a lethal virus
    To be appalled by the build up of nuclear weapons
    To see the promotion of fossil fuels, not renewables
    To feel anxious over the impulsiveness of each day
    To absorb the lies, distractions, and meanness
    To lower the expectations of an empire in chaos

And the list goes on and so will the pendulum
    Between progress or law and order
    Between truth and misinformation
    Between protests and a police state
    Between nonviolence and forceful control
    Between creation and destruction
    Between speaking up or silence on injustices

Forgive our anger for how it all turns out or doesn't
    A few might find courage to show remorse
    How complicit we are in writing history books
    Who and what we love will endure.

> *6/9/20 (On occasion when a persistent protest hit the streets in memory of George Floyd, which resisted racism and caused deep pain in how we arrived at this place in history)*

Sunset of Discontent

America is returning to the '60s
    When the chaos of the streets
    Was reacting to Vietnam and
    The law and order of a Nixon era
Yet movements were created
    That addressed the "isms" of progress
    Such as the anti-war movement
        Civil rights against slavery
        Feminism and women's equality
        Abortion and reproductive choices
        Gender and LGBTQ rights
        Militarism and nuclear weapons
        Environmentalism and Earth Day
        Labor laws and corporate power
The acceleration of 60 years changes
    The way we view the world
    Without a cold war mentality
    How we connect with computers
    The way we raise our children
    How we relate sexually as male-female
    The way we think about spirituality
    And the cosmic view of space travel
Now in a pandemic stricken milieu
    America wears a mask to hide its fears
    Threatened by right-wing militant forces
    On the verge of becoming a police state
    Having elected an authoritarian leader
    Who is impeachable and sociopathic
    Spawning hordes of anger out on the streets

Dark shadows fall on the sunset of discontent
    Waiting for an election of a different leader
    Who will mend a dismantled democracy
    Unleashing the sunrise of life and liberty.

6/2/20 (On occasion when massive protests saw America moving through a transition of pandemic and police control in the death of George Floyd)

Not So Happy Fourth

We have reached a peculiar time
   in America on this Fourth of July
   when we are besieged by three attacks
   of a pandemic, poverty, and racism

These overwhelming forces immobilize
   America to its knees, some to pray
   others to concede that we have problems
   requiring change to this historic moment

No one was quite prepared for COVID-19
   but soon we were hiding behind masks
   and measuring six feet from each other
   scared of the sky-rocketing statistics

The most vulnerable are often poor people
   who work in clusters of close conditions
   failing to have adequate health insurance
   feeling the economic dip of unemployment

Sustained protests burst on the streets even
   after George Floyd pleaded, "I can't breathe"
   neither could a nation breathe any more racism
   and the symbols of confederacy came down

In the midst of this chaos was a President
   who denied the impact of the coronavirus
   telling us how it would magically disappear
   blustering forth with how wonderful he is

The traditional gathering, grilling, fireworks
    meant a different focus on the Constitution
    not based on superiority of white Trumpers
    but accepting that diversity is created equal.

> *(On occasion of reaching the Fourth of July during this era with misgivings or a sad realization of its historic significance)*

Fright and Flight

It's making us sick
    The cases are unbelievably frightening
    More than 10,000 per day in some States
But it's not only the coronavirus
    It is the cavalier attitude of the unmasked
    Those who put economics before safety
It's feeling the moment
    Being here with a level of sadness
    Yet feeling thrilled to be alive
Attentive to a pin prick, a beautiful meal
    A twisted pun, a successful project
    A restful nap, a well-shaped poem
Hearing the news when the Dakota pipeline
    Was shut down after the Standing Rock
    Sioux Tribe protested a right to sacred land
Or seeing books expose the incompetence
    Of President Donald Trump who has failed
    To act coherently in his reaction to COVID-19
A robin visits a branch outside my window
    On a hot summer day with lots of sunshine
    The flight of a bird frees my exuberance.

> 7/9/20 *(On occasion of feeling good during the pandemic after learning that a court order ceased oil production that infringed on the Standing Rock environmental concerns)*

Stop the Merry-Go-Round

We would welcome each new day
With soothing music
To take our mind off
The mounting deaths
The merry noise of deceitful voices
That wouldtry to suppress Medicaid
That is careless about COVID-19
Trampling on institutions like the CDC
Dismantling the Affordable Care Act
Trying to do away with Social Security
Stop the noise; it is making us dizzy

They spread unhealthy policies
Militarism of superfluous missiles
Racism and fascism and dictatorship
Generating deep rifts of division
Attacking the science of climate change
Stop the noise; it is making us dizzy

Values that were dear to our democracy
Are being challenged by a chaotic election
And degrading a nation's moral principles
Stop the noise; it is making us dizzy

How low can we go as a nation in limbo?
As rich gets richer and poor gets poorer
As the Prez of Chaos goes in a tailspin
We must get off this dizzy merry-go-round.

Legal Intent

The virus is quickly spreading
    But not in the way the President intends
    For the Supreme Court issues viral news
    That no President is above the law
Everybody knew that except this President
    Who has skewed the legal boundaries
    By firing his opposition, withholding taxes
    Denying the virus, giving false information
In affirming the three branches of government
    Congress called for executive accountability
    And the Supreme Court asserted independence
    Restoring the intent of separate institutions
Now what is missing is enforcing the law
    Over a President who intends to make a mess
    In every way possible to get re-elected
    By understating a vision for democracy
Will we ever restore a vision for peace
    With trust in our allies and coping with a virus
    And see justice in eliminating the virus of racism
    And find fair elections for healthy leadership?

7/10/20 (On occasion when the Supreme Court made a number of positive pronouncements at a low point in the history of this Republic)

Sad Storms

A persistent rain storm bombards Kansas City
pouring into the basement with wet insistence
leaving drops of sadness on the trembling leaves
calling out CT Vivian, John Lewis, Mary Trump

This last one who wrote a book set off alarms
to alert voters about foreboding dangers
confirming what we have felt all along
that her impeached Uncle is unfit for office

The storm of the weekend was the coronavirus
dripping with statistics of pervasive death
while the White House hides in a nostalgic bubble
claiming this reign of terror will magically disappear

The answer is not to send troops to Portland
to squelch violence by providing more violence
but to follow in the footsteps of John Lewis
to march forward against fascism and racism.

> *7/20/20 (On occasion of a frenzied weekend that saw the deaths of Rep. John Lewis, Pastor CT Vivian, noted preacher and civil rights leader, plus the courageous move of Mary Trump to come out with a sad narrative about a dictatorial and racist President)*

Limbo

Getting low enough to win
Seems the goal of this Presidency
Who has detached reality
From any common decency
Now he sends unmarked Fed spies
Into Portlandia to kidnap protestors
Who simply are confronting racism
And the extent of violence by police

He has a distaste for masks
That might mess up his hair
In the face of scientific evidence
That masks are a virus prescription
He has a need to relish the opposite
Assuring that he will be the "bad boy"
In a twisted logic of contradictions
Seeking attention for negative behavior

He loves his sociopathic power
Keeping the timid off guard with threats
And watching them scurry to escape
His "firings" mistaking fear for respect
He covers the truth with bold face lies
Embellishing his signature with a flourish
Slipping into nostalgic grandiose projections
Only for us to wonder how low he can go.

7/22/20 (On occasion when the pandemic is getting worse with little national leadership from President Trump and review this time as a low point in the history of the U.S.)

Face Up

Show us honesty
    To stop pretending
        That you care
When you can't stand up
    For those who are poor
    Or get behind health care
    Or include immigrants
Show us who you really are
    Rather than coded language
        Hiding the truth of your intent
            Making us think you care
Quit hiding, stop the games
    Be authentic, be courageous
    By starting to be honest.

(On occasion during the presidential pandemic when the White House and his party have a problem being honest)

Poems Instead of Plagues

COVID-19 creeps into the tangled jungle
    Like a venomous snake striking its prey
    Unsuspecting victims of an invisible force

President45 snarls loudly like a hungry tiger
    Ready to pounce upon vulnerable victims
    Rendering them food for political gain

Both plagues are dangerous carnivores
    Leaving behind a trail of mayhem and fear
    Confusing any plans to control the damage

If one had a poem like a slingshot on Goliath
    What stone or word would make a difference
    Since the destruction has already happened?

A poem might appeal to a higher consciousness
    Like putting on a mask or waiting for an election
    By getting ready for the next line of defense

Plagues pass into history but a poem endures
    Bringing out the best part of the human spirit
    Delivering the maximum return for survival.

        7/30/20 (On occasion of reading a tiny thing like a poem for courage
        while plagues eventually pass into the judgment of history)

Duped

Magic shows are fascinating
    Even when you know the trick
    Mesmerized by naive gullibility
Some easily fall for the distractions
    Caught up in the story, fabricated
    We want to believe the messenger
Unfortunately some really are lying
    Entertainers who are uneducated
    And fail to fact check their sources
Even smart people might drink Kool Aid
    If they are caught in a personality cult
    Unprepared for critical thinking
American Exceptionalism grips a nation
    As it confronts a magical election
    Shame on this cult of dubious choice.

(On occasion of disbelief in the herd instinct of Trump followers at the GOP convention)

Poem About Trump and COVID-19

The thing is
    There must be a breakdown
        Somewhere between life and death
COVID-19 searches for ways
    To take advantage
        Of access to receptive bodies
Places that show little resistance
    Where the immune system
        Or a vaccine is unavailable
The point of assault
    Was already prepared
        By an atmosphere of Trumpism
Who created a series of breakdowns
    By disorganizing institutions
        Setting up unhealthy levels of stress
It was as if a wrecking ball
    Was moving through a nation
        Destroying everything in its path
So that the nation was a prime target
    To become a victim of an insidious attack
        By a silent invisible formidable killer
Pouncing haphazardly on happy-go-lucky
    Individuals without a care in the world
        In naive denial of scientific precautions
We might ignore lessons of another era
    When Nero fiddled away while Rome burned
        But at great peril we could self-destruct

Whenever we stockpile powerful missiles
    That could compound Hiroshima to exhaust
        And end the human enterprise as we know it
Elections have consequences in a democracy
    Paying heed to nuclear weapons and climate
        Survival by first promoting life over death.

8/18/20 (On occasion of checking our election savvy by asking if Trumpism promotes more destruction than life)

Crazy Day

this turns out to be another day of insanity
when words are ravaged into mush
and truth is no longer meaningful
when all references fail normal communication

then you actually meet a Trumper
who trumpets nonsense from Fox News
and you want to listen and respect their view
but later conclude that they are still unaware

frustrating when things are not going well
the coronavirus has spread out of control
and the White House is inept in its response
and the computer is making one go crazy

time for a vacation or a nap or to seek help
or to admit that some things are beyond us
so we wait out the virus, let go of our rage
and recharge an attempt to find the password.

(On occasion of trying to turn around the craziness by finding the right password)

Hurt in America

COVID-19 has defeated us
Except New York every state suffers
From extreme defiance of science
As individual misinformation prevails

America is hurting right now

Families have reason to worry
About the rising deaths, about school
Paying bills, facing evictions, eating
Over leadership boosting false narratives

America is hurting right now

People go to virtual church for answers
Receiving the comfort of a good God
Who will make everything okay in the end
But disturbing questions still persist

America is hurting right now

It is time to learn humility that is real
An honesty about a system that lives in a bubble
Needing new ideas about health care and democracy
Going to vote not repeating the same mistakes

America is hurting right now. "Make good trouble."

(On occasion of wondering if America can recover from the coronavirus. John Lewis said, "Make good trouble.")

A New Day

The music unfolds in easy waves
    In overlapping melodies of delight
    Settling into the sands of serenity
    That perhaps we can recover the soul
    Of a nation besieged by angry division

The pick of Kamala Harris as Biden's Veep
    Starts the process of restoring a vision
    And cleansing the nation of bad policy
    Gripped by twisted conspiracy theories
    And paralyzed ineptitude toward COVID-19

The Democratic Convention will realize
    Key leadership positions for the next election
    To set the Biden-Harris team in motion
    And climb out of this deep pit of regression
    Where stupidity and cruelty have ruled the day.

8/13/20 (On occasion when Joe Biden carefully vetted a running mate to answer the call to bring variety and hope in a transfer of leadership)

Con Games

A well-oiled salesman dominated the GOP
    As the greatest con man of any White House
    Gathering a gang of gangsters around him
Many who have flaunted the rule of law
    Engaging in dishonest behavior as criminals
    Spreading the con game throughout the party
The confluence of scandal and a code of silence
    Supported the deceptive schemes of the con artist
    So business went on with "do nothing" results
Complicit are the voters who were easily conned
    Taking the bait and maintaining their loyalty
    Receiving distorted information from Fox News
Some were duped when they failed critical thinking
    Following along blindly any right-wing position
    Undermining the forward changes of a nation.

8/22/20 (On occasion between the two party conventions where the choice is starkly contrasted but needs an election to unite a better purpose)

Correcting a Mistake

    Intimate mindfulness
Over political distance
    Smart safety
Over pandemic distance
    Thoughtful voting
Forwards progression
    Empathy for the poor
Embraces love and peace.

    (On occasion of waiting for November 3, 2020 to correct a mistake)

Misplaced

Why can't people get it right?
    A lot of them defend police
    Even when they shoot Jacob Blake
    In the back in front of the kids
Yet the police will allow a teenager
    To wildly display his rifle after
    He shot two protesters concluding
    Protesters are bad. Not police cruelty
On and on it goes in the White House
    Where Black Lives don't Matter
    In the case of choking George Floyd
    In countless cases of peaceful protesters
Put a gun in the hands of fearful police
    And they make terrible choices on control
    Thinking they have to use them on Blacks
    They misplace violence for more violence
Why can't we get it right?
    We have a mess on our hands
    And getting more guns is not the answer
    How do we change this culture of violence?

8/30/20 (On occasion of addressing the issue of violence with gun control and less fear)

What is Wrong with People?

When Donald J. Trump was first put in office
    I was thrown into a deep paralysis of shock
    Wincing in pain like a martyr on the cross
    ". . . they know not what they are doing"
    Yet I was not ready to forgive them
    But rather to cry out, "How could they
    Be complicit in ruining a nation and reverse
    Every worthwhile value that made sense to me?"
Sometimes I'm just angry, sometimes just numb
    Not knowing what to say to an iceberg
    Which is like talking to Trump supporters
    Who have formed a monolithic cult
    Who are unwavering in sinking any Titanic
    Boat of progressive ideas and democratic ideals
    Just coldly indifferent in melting a conflict
    That would cause the impasse of a fatal division
Both sides have enough anger to go around
    Providing a basis for civil discussion except
    When QAnon, conspiracy lies, Boogaloos
    Attaching themselves to right-wing issues
    Like anti-abortion and gun advocacy offering
    One–sided issues that fail to find any resolution
    Even by an Election or Supreme Court decision

We are in trouble unless we can soften our pride
    Find a way to come together on a common vision
    Admit the disconnect in losing to the pandemic
    Turn around our selfishness to some higher values
    Learn to think critically by listening to each other
    Accept our vulnerability to melt any icebergs in us
    And if it would help, I'd say it, "God help us all."

        9/7/20 (On occasion on finding myself vulnerable to the chaos
        of a Black Lives Matter and Trump era and resolving
        to make things better after the next election)

What Have We Done to Ourselves?

We have tied ourselves up
    In a convoluted entanglement

What have they achieved from 911?
    But ruination in endless war and revenge
    Amassing a military budget of 800 Billion
    Shifting away resources meant to tackle climate change
    Burning up the environment in red partisanship
    Turning to violent embarrassment and division
    Jeopardizing a democracy for a dictatorship

When will we come to our senses?
    Rediscovering the tender yearning for peace
    Standing for justice where Black Lives Matter
    Caring for Creation to confront climate change
    Developing an openness to avoid rigid legalism
    Striving for higher values to be honestly authentic
    Forming compassionate communities showing love

Can we? Will we? To our last breath, help us live.

        9/12/20 (On occasion a day after the 19th Anniversary of 911 and a
        virtual birthday for grandchildren to carry on a forward legacy)

Catatonic

Everything came to a halt
Like the death of a society
Ceasing hyperactive breathing
Slowing down to a palpitation
To outlast the wave of fear
Before reviving fun engagement
Like joining a population surge

Most kept their six-foot distance
By checking phones and Wi-Fi
And watching a lot of TV
Until COVID-19 passed over
The precipice of a fatal fall

Lessons of a pandemic teach us
To follow the warning of scientists
To care for the vulnerable ones
To find solace in our time alone
To choose wisely our fun events
To avoid a nuclear holocaust
To avert climate destruction
To counter a state of ignorance
To give thanks for surviving "now."

*(On occasion of an historic moment when the
entire world was coping with coronavirus)*

Corona Insights

What I rediscovered in the coronavirus
    Beyond the threat of climate change fires
    And the shock from daily counts of death
Tis the thankfulness to be alive
    And to feel the security of retirement
    To find the perfect job that fulfills
The freedom to do what matters to you
    To luxuriate in the wonder of thought
    To catch those flighty words in poetry
To listen to music that wanders in my mind
    That quietly resonates to my soul center
    Giving a peace that passes understanding
To find communion in an intimate embrace
    With my beloved mate in a special passion
    Of the greatest love story of two destinies
To taste delicious dining with sensual pleasure
    To feel the joy of one's place in family
    And experience the seasons of beauty
Even to endure the distance of one's neighbors
    To shut down their noise with headphones
    And escape the wider violence of division
To realize that one is helpless to change others
    Who are set in their ways of being so right
    About single issues like abortion and guns
COVID-19 teaches us a lesson in patience
    To accept the limitation of stubborn progress
    In bending the arc of the universe toward justice

To die in the yearning of the next generation
   To await the verdict of unforeseen survival
   If to be alive is to tip the balance toward love.

> *9/15/20 (On occasion of putting a pause on our protest and restlessness to find hope if we are still alive after a Black Lives Matter and coronavirus era)*

Trumptations

So he actually said something unpatriotic
   That the warriors of the military were "losers"
   For fighting in endless wars and the generals
   Were only interested in weapon profiteering
The Prez of Chaos actually blurted this publicly
   However much he denied this campaign blunder
   Not even the peace movement would admit this
   Because of the sincerity of the many sacrifices
Thus some questions are raised in this admission
   If one sees a nation's greatness by military might
   Or by how well a nation takes care of the poor
   Or affirms the arts and welfare of the people
Followers of the mindset of this chaos are conned
   Into the illusion of missiles and economic priorities
   When the measure of a nation's soul is about caring
   Policies of racial justice, peacemaking, earth repair
Even if there is a sliver of truth to what he says
   He thinks he's smarter than other "suckers
   That prepare for war in the military complex
   Really the name-calling sticks better with him.

> *9/9/20 (On occasion of analyzing the reelection campaign of the Prez of Chaos, who called soldiers "losers," which turns out to be his greatest blunder smacking against a sacred foundation of patriotism)*

Hide the Masks (Hypocrisy)

Easy being a right-winger
A Trump supporter
Go along with the crowd
Take the easiest path

Accept the status quo
Follow Fox News
Bet on what you see
Never ask probing questions

Basically be uneducated
Learn to survive
Follow an authority
Do not uncover deeper truths

Be merry on the merry-go-round
Look out for your family
But don't care for the poor
Support policies of the GOP

Back it up with a gun
In case someone disagrees
Remember you're always right
Keep it simple.

9/26/20 (On occasion of frustration when listening to both sides produces no forum for discussion. Of course, saying this does not help cross the divide)

Dead End

Disastrous debate
National embarrassment
Sad culmination of bluster
By this madman and his deceit

The disgruntled joined a caravan
Leading into a maze of wrong turns
Culminating in a traffic jam
And dead-end disappointment

The wreckage leaves a messy trail
Of racism, fascism and authoritarianism
Packed together by fear and ruination
Of the fragile ideal of democracy

This and the pandemic is taking its toll
Perhaps many will come to their senses
And escape to go vote in an election
To undo what has been undone.

10/1/20 (On occasion of assessing the first debate of Trump and Biden, "Heavy on insults, light on substance.")

Karma

Out of the dizziness
    Came the shocking news
    The President is a victim
    Of a "no masks" rally
Touting his toughness
    As a hidden white supremacist
    He appeared to be immune
    To ordinary vulnerability
His supporters followed
    His leadership of taunting
    The massacre of thousands
    Defying masks and distancing
While no one can bully this virus
    The irony is that COVID-19 won
    In a ruthless display of Karma
    What goes around, comes around
We need change to be accountable
    A right wing culture is unacceptable
    Less force and more kindness
    Empathetic leadership and masks.

10/2/20 (On occasion in making sense of dizzy events and dealing with the coronavirus)

Conspiracy Consumers

Conspiracy consumers
Distort reality
Feeding excitement
For misinformation

Gobbling up Fox News
And conservative social media
Suspicious of main line news
Projecting a voice of authority

No wonder that democracy
Leans toward right-wing bias
Surely not wearing a mask
Is defiantly more exotic

The polarities are defined
The truth is disputed
You fight for your own way
Ignoring a greater truth

Without honesty we are confused
We stick our heads in the sand
We join flat earth pretenders
We are being driven without headlights.

10/5/20 (On occasion when conspiracy theories undermined the wearing of masks during the pandemic by questioning the science of truth-telling)

Fly Bye

Millions tuned into the debate
    Between VP Pence and Senator Harris
Speculating about a fly landing
    On Pence's head for two and half minutes
An enormous amount of time to wonder
    If he would "swallow the fly, perhaps
    He'll die," given the number of deaths
    From the COVID-19 debacle and chaos
This "fly-by-nite" prevaricator mocks us
    By believing if you vote for me
    You get to take from me my health care
    You get to have my social security
    You can suppress my mail-in vote
    You can deny the science of the climate
    You can build a wall we do not need
    You can add another unnecessary missile
    You can load up more AK47s for massacres
    You can pass tax cuts for the rich not the poor
    You can sneak in judges to undo LGBTQ rights
    You can degrade our international diplomacy
    You use cognitive dissonance for contradictions
    You approve police brutality not peace protestors
The list is longer than the number of eyes on a fly
    That discerns more truth than from a myopic world.

                10/8/20 (On occasion of rating the Vice Presidential Debates:
                                Harris No. 1 and The Fly No. 2)

Headed into the Fall

It's shivering outside
Patches of snow hide
Between outstretched arms
Of huddling maple trees
Except for one standing alone
Cuddled in orange flames
By the frigid pond

The election is heated up
By pandemic stricken lines
Waiting to exercise their vote
While the Prez of Chaos
Pontificates at his rallies
Bragging about his cleverness
In sneaking in a literalistic judge
To do his manic-fire bidding
To consume red states
Under an orange crown
With no mask for trick or treating

Halloween would come early
But his Fall would come later
As many more would die
Insisting they lost by trickery
And so the pretense would pass
And the lies would face the truth
That we could pick up pieces
Out of the candy-coated Fall.

(On occasion of facing an election on November 3, 2020 that ended a national nightmare that is still scary and divisive)

Conundrum

It just defies human logic
How followers of the Trump
Become super stupor spreaders
Attending rallies with no masks
Unquestioning the President
Making up story after story
Without a clue of what is required
To be President of a great nation
Before a nation is degraded
By the curse of incompetence
And the need to win at all costs

I guess it has to do with context
An ability to look more deeply
For the soul behind appearances
To see substance behind the façade
To care about things that matter

Context would examine maturity
In allowing a spiritual depth
In breathing in beauty around us
In using words that elevate
In contributing to a better world
In enhancing loving relationships
In allowing space for others to grow
In becoming a fun person to be around
In being less controlling and difficult
In being aware between birth and death.

*10/29/20 (On occasion of wondering how so many people
never raise questions about their leaders)*

Eye on an Election

The eye of the hurricane
Never loses speed
From the beginning to the end
Carving a path of destruction

The eye is an ego of indulgence
Of four years in the White House
Reversing every sensible value
Substituting double-speak talk

Truth is in the eyes of the beholder
Making up one's own reality
Verified by one's own cult
Outside main-line thinking

Suddenly words lose meaning
Repeated enough times lies seem real
Concepts disappear like conservatism
Threats like a virus no longer exist

All is chaos in an alternate universe
No longer a common norm, just division
Attacking the other side to win an election
Hoping my solution is one protest vote.

> 11/3/20 (On occasion when different perspectives on the election can change
> the dynamics of a democracy from using forceful measures,
> Separating children in cages, trashing the rights of mainline media
> Flaunting impeachment hearings, ignoring plans to fight the pandemic
> Elevating status quo above protests, attacking people for disloyalty,
> in finding common ground to go forward, even though that may be hard to do)

Protest Vote

Finally my protest vote
Having endured the Trump debacle
Even as he resonates to many
I guess it has always been a protest
Against certain elements of patriotism

I prefer peace
Not law and order
Not nationalism
Not militarism
Not tough guy bullying

I understand immigrants
Who appreciate those things
When they haven't had safety
They are proud of a nation
Calling for freedom from dictatorship
But I would caution their loyalties

Democracy has double-edged meanings
As a nation of laws protecting equal rights
But it also protects minorities
To have access to the American dream
Both rich and poor, justice for both citizens
Whereby the haves do not exclude the have-nots

A citizen needs to make choices of parties
Discerning when one party tries to over-control
Exerting superiority over another
By racist attitudes, by divisive policies
By strong arm tactics with weapons
Violence and slavery are unacceptable

Voting is a sacred act of citizenship
Who looks deeper into the "context"
In what's behind the appearance of things
Using critical thinking to analyze policy
That uplifts the poor and lessens harmful weapons
That knows the difference
Between the status quo and progressives
That strives for higher values beyond survival
That undergirds life over death.

My protest vote is a statement of spiritual values.

11/3/20 (On occasion of making one of my most important votes even if it is a minority vote of one vote for a democracy)

Biden Says, "Bye Don"

Only a few fragile leaves
Held hands with bare arms
Of majestic maples
Changing colors
In the annual display
Of the fall season

Four days on a Saturday
After the election count
Pennsylvania hired Joe
Closing down the dark days
Of the Trump presidency
Letting light filter
Through the naked skeletons

The stress succumbed
To relief as throngs of people
Poured out dancing in the streets
A new day was declared
Aspiring to tall trees
Holding their heads high
Like steeples shouting
Their prayers to the heavens.

11/8/20 (On occasion when the fall election of November 3, 2020 filtered the nightmare of America's ordeal with a confluence of seventy million chaotic disagreements, over 100,000 record number of COVID-19 cases and a huge intake of oxygen relief)

A Ghost in the White House

A ghost of an evil specter
   haunts a clammy closet
      of the White House
and can be heard
   at three in the morning
      in tweety clicking sounds
that make inane comments
   about cultural trivia
      in boasting tough threats
and once in awhile
   leaves its familiar zone
      to go overseas
to make huge arm deals
   to set up a dangerous future
      for threatening civil wars

Who will make America scary again
   Or expose a skeleton of brittle ideas?
      Time to clean out the closet.

(On occasion of seeing a pattern of laying the groundwork of authoritarian leadership)

Loyalty to a Cult

Spell bound and numbed and fearful
Voters surrendered critical thinking
By following an entertaining personality
Rather than searching for higher values
Soon they were caught up in a cult
Ignoring society's destruction and their own.

*(On occasion of watching the dismantling of
values in following the chaos of Trump)*

Canyon

I feel sadness for division
For all the COVID-19 victims
As rain falls on my window
Clouding the view of my backyard
Streaming in steamy droplets
From my room full of shadows
As I ponder if I was too harsh
On this Prez of Chaos
Whom on the one hand I despair
Over the ruination of this nation
Complicit by the foggy illusion
Of his deniers and Proud Boys
Who will never concede an election

On the other hand I feel relief
That we can return to normal
Functioning in solving problems
Revitalizing the tiredness of COVID-19
Preparing for a hopeful message
In a season of surprise again
When Christmas can be special

The "corona" exposed vulnerabilities
In a nation pictured with miles of cars
Waiting for food and spiritual hunger
Seeking answers to the scourge of death
Alone in hospital beds from loved ones
Grasping for crumbs from breaking bread
Living an illusion after denying an election
Yet the cup of salvation will pour a stream

Of hope to the four corners of the earth
As the wind of change restores movement
Selecting a baton after four years of chaos
If only we can turn our eyes from chasm
United to see the wonder of a Grand Canyon.

> *11/26/20 (On occasion in seeing deep division caused by an election, the coronavirus, tiredness, relief, and a way to look forward through Christmas eyes of Canyon beauty, Jeremy's birthday on Thanksgiving and Jesus's on Christmas, and bountiful blessings)*

Democracy In Jeopardy

The stark reality of this winter day
Is stillness even with a slight breeze
In the top of gargoyle-like stiff trees
Splitting the grey humdrum boring sky
It's like this for many people's lives
Without much change, just routine
So when a spectacle like Trump appears
An excess of excitement fills the void
The landscape of politics alters reality
Shifting from two parties to three
With the addition of a Trump Party
As a haven for right-wing conspiracies
The classical understanding of liberals
Was to be open to change and other opinions
Which fit nicely into the party of Democrats
To replace some previous ways of thinking
What bothers liberals is the shortsightedness
Of the GOP and Trump Party to change
And learn some new progressive ideas
Which have less illusion and more honesty
If the parties could come and listen together
Respecting a democracy of We the People
Rather than an autocracy that controls others
Then we could feel the warmth of going forward.

12/11/20 (On occasion when 126 members of congress seditiously broke away from the two parties to overturn an election confirmed by a 9 to 0 Supreme Court decision)

Chasing Hope

The scab of a wounded nation
Is being peeled off deliberately
Leaving a scar as an ugly reminder
That we are flawed and imperfect

The stark reality of a death wish
Makes lonely trees look brittle and cold
During the final gasps of four years
When the pandemic rampages over life

Contested elections and five executions
Reveal a fragile atmosphere of violence
In the entertainment before Inauguration
Before an administration begins to be well

Now is the time to do something—
Much easier when talking to core values
Like people with peace, justice, ecology,
Openness, authenticity, love in their lives
More difficult with those entrenched in
Right-wing conspiracy theories, literalism,
Hypocrisy, control through patriotism

Warming the transition are colored lights
Hung on trees inside homes shining through
The doubts and fears of a shivering nation
While outside squirrels chase hope around.

11/30/20 (On occasion of an Amy Goodman report that the Trump administration has allowed the schedule of five executions, mostly black and one woman, before going out of office, which has not occurred in 100 years, signaling its propensity for violence)

Momentum in December

On a Monday the Fourteenth
Vaccine delivered COVID relief
A shot in the arm to stop the spread
The Electoral College confirmed
The end of a national nightmare

I have a secret confession
I liked enduring the corona era
I didn't worry about what I wore
I could find time to write
I feasted on sumptuous dining
I reduced scheduling meetings
I was in shorts during virtual church
I could enjoy the intimacy of home
I could work on some projects
I spent less money on travel
I had time to think and meditate
I had the luxury of leisure
I didn't have to hear the GOP lies
I could see some evolve to greater truth
I analyzed the Stupor Spreader
I dealt with anger for ruining a nation
But admittedly I felt the pain
Of innocent victims facing death
Missing some of my friends
Others snagged in the cult of fear

Remnants of the nightmare will go on
But so will some signs of democracy
The heartthrobs of a nation are fragile
Gratefully the Fourteenth gave us a pulse.

> *12/16/20 (On occasion when an historic moment can see the promise of a vaccine and we can revive the energy of competent leadership. Lucky are any of us if we survive)*

The Trump Stump

The most farfetched thought
Trump could be reelected!
It happened once
When people were deceived
Into the convenience of a cult

Here is the business model
That makes executive decisions
Using Presidential executive powers
Without checking on others
And avoiding a sense of cooperation
And compassion for policy choices

He runs around from court to court
Trying to manipulate a big lie
To stay in power when he lost
Making people go Holiday crazy
It baffles the imagination!

Christmas is an unprecedented time
Reminding us to leave behind King Herod
And give birth to a new spirit again
Of love and peace and star-like vision.

> *12/21/20 (On occasion of perishing the thought that an accidental repeat could replace democracy with a monarchy)*

Hidden Divide

It will take a leap of faith
To move from literalism
To higher criticism

Likewise it takes education
To graduate from survival needs
As in Maslow's hierarchy
To a higher level of authenticity

These two principles
Are hidden from most people
In the growth and development
Of a human being
And are behind the Great Divide
Between conservatism
    and liberals
Between an imaginative faith
    and social justice
Between the status quo
    and progressives

Crossing the Great Divide
    requires honesty
And the shedding of hypocrisy
Looking for openings
    and conversations
        for common ground.

Strands

Strings, threads, strands
Link us to an invisible connection
Tying us to a legacy of a small star
And a cosmic community

Humankind has entered dark ages
Where demonic scissors clip ties
To normal flight and cooperation
Between right and left wings

Domestic terrorism has exposed
A canyon that divides two sides
Of America, both forceful and gentle
That together can be beautifully grand

Police are called to rein in violence
To protect law and order forcefully
But show an affinity to right-wingers
Still confused by peaceful protesters

Left-wingers are open to change
And easily adopt the peace movement
While right-wingers allow for hate groups
And idolize the Flag as an ultimate concern

A fake reality is a threat to democracy
Lies, conspiracy, cults, brainwashing
Hide the truth, particularly the second truth
Whereby one can unlearn for deeper truths

The strands of democracy are in upheaval
Catapulted by right-wing violence
And the push of liberal idealism
Each straining to find life over death.

> *1/12/21 (On occasion in reflecting on the coup of January 6, 2021, the second impeachment of the President on January 13, 2021 and what he will do before the Inauguration on January 20, 2021)*

A Christmas Nightmare

'Twas the night before Christmas
After the foggy election of Biden-Harris
When the Donald sat alone in his office
    Putting a pipe to his mouth
    Puffing out a cloud of smoke
    Drifting into a dream
    Reliving every rally in his head
Haunted by apparitions of images
    Of former staffers he had fired
As the room turned dark and gloomy
    Suddenly revealing ghostly figures
    Who spoke in accusatory whispers

The first Ghost swirled like a hurricane
Spewing water into the oval sealed room
So that the Donald was rising to the top
Gasping for air from the fear of drowning
As he cried for help then a voice gurgled,
"I'm here to remind you that I am
The Ghost of Floods, a frequent visitor
To the Gulf of Mexico causing terror
By the names of Laura, Delta, and Dennis
Each having devastating results like Katrina
Like Noah of Biblical times with few spared.
So why spare you when you show a cavalier
Attitude during Maria by tossing paper towels?"

The second Ghost, COVID-19, spared no mercy
Infesting the globe with a lethal virus
Particularly targeting the unmasked Americans
Most notably the leader of the free world

Who arrogantly defied the science of prevention
Jeopardizing more lives than all the wars before
Defining an era of before or after the corona
The voice of COVID-19 sounded apologetic,
"You know, Donald, you degraded yourself
And nation by becoming a poor example."
The present moment felt enormous pain.

The third Ghost, Fire, flickered before sunrise
Mesmerized by the warm glowing fireplace
Spreading the searing flame from log to log
Like the raging fires in the forests of California
Which left questions about future devastation
Of a presidency leaving ashes on a democracy
    Increasing the flames of racism and division
    Stoking the fire of misinformation over conception
    Denying the science of climate change
    Exasperating the nuclear threat to end life
    Causing loss of life by modeling no masks
    Undermining education by promoting literalism
    Developing a cult of personality requiring loyalty
    Stacking the Supreme Court with conservatives
    Building walls to keep out undesirable immigrants

This Ghost turned Donald into a fantasy ball of fire
    Snorting and screaming about a fraudulent election
    Consuming the hot air into a crematory powder
    Dismissing the GOP for a right-wing Trump Party
    Signaling an accident in history or horrific dream
    It was over now or just continuing illusions of chaos
    Still, Joe Biden was made for this historic moment
    When the dust settles one can hear children stirring
    Waking up to the morning sun with gifts of wonder.

(On occasion of following the presidential cycle of Donald J. Trump between the years of 2017–2021, based on the tale of A Christmas Carol by Charles Dickens)

Insurrection

Danger, threats, impeachment
Are reactions to a coup on democracy

The angry nail on the coffin of Trumpism
Calls for accountability on a riotous mob

Four years of lies, lies, lies have disrupted
The calm surface of exhausting racism

That promotes the Electoral College
A tiresome trapping of white privilege

It's baffling why we endure over 1,000 hate groups
That force domestic terrorism on the rest of us

Proud Boys want to destroy the government
They want to hold onto white supremacy

A massive security failure succumbed
To overwhelming numbers of aggression

Appeasement to a white mob was allowable
If it were blacks and browns, probably a bloodbath

This is America, this is US, this is the Eagle
This is militarism, this is boot camp parenting

So a lot of people believe in conspiracy theories
Believing in nationalism, believing in self-serving

During the endgame, Trump incited violence
And aroused an impeachment hearing, again

Something will have to change a cultish atmosphere
To breathe out peace, justice and creation

Something could uplift a spiritual set of values
To breathe in openness, authenticity, and love

Then will we believe in pursuing truth over lies
How refreshing that can feel in a new administration.

> *1/7/21 (On occasion of tracing the saga of the 45th President, after four exhausting years, and after a mob desecrated the Capitol during the certification meeting of the Electoral College on January 6, 2021, then flowing into the virtual joy of January 20, 2021, to celebrate a Code Blue rescue of Democracy)*

End of an Era

The Presidential pandemic
    Has left the country
    Extremely polarized
    Fearful, biased, masked

Many say 2020 is the worst year
    Since the coronavirus rings out
    A higher death toll than any war
    A daily toll equal to 911

Yet the country is far larger
    Than any one individual
    And pockets of creativity
    Surpass any negativity of one

The country has had to absorb a shock
    To a system demanding justice and peace
    Watching leadership take us down
    A path that has degraded our values

Black Lives Matter broke through
    A consciousness that shifted hearts
    The racism in this white society
    That missed the intent of the marchers

By organizing, Georgia saved democratic values
    Causing a 50/50 Senate split on January 6, 2021
    And offering a new majority leader the gateway
    For voting on impending legislation for a new era

Endings are often messier than beginnings
    Desperate was Trump to recall an election
    As he manipulated delusional fantasies
    Culminating in a coup attacking the Capitol

This has been the ultimate disappointment
    In observing loyalists who blindly voted
    And followed the besmirching of America
    By degrading the essence of democracy

The Prez of Chaos has generated
    Delay, anger, stupor, hardship
    Opposition in a fragile democracy

Can this be a launchpad for the best of times?

(On occasion in marking the end of an era of chaos and a change of Presidential leadership on January 20, 2021)

Impeached–Again!

In one of the quirks of history
The Prez of Chaos was impeached
As his support fell away
With his empire collapsing

He lost his tweeter voice
Propagating the Big Lie about the election
As he became unhinged in psycho-babble
Denying culpability for the coup

Americans were also falling into an abyss
Experiencing resignation, exhausted over
The pandemic, no work, no food, no rent
A cultural loss of indigenous people

It came to a second impeachment
From his betrayal of the Constitution
Hanging onto a frayed thread of power
Stretching apart the seams of democracy

Trump left a legacy of two impeachments
Following him around like a red letter A
Dogged by civil suits and court hearings
If only everyone's mirror could reverse things

Never again lessons revealed the lies of a mob
Desperately needing recognition and acceptance
Adopting authoritarianism over democracy
Putting superficial patriotism over a deeper truth

Yet sadness must follow the coup and the trial
How so many found themselves on the wrong track
Hoping to look for a light at the end of a tunnel
Only to meet an approaching light of the Trump train.

> *1/19/21 (On occasion when the four year legacy of Trump ended in the Empire's propensity for death, providing some relief to go forward)*

Postscript: A Beautiful Day

I didn't know if I would see this day
A reversal of all the negativity of four years
It feels so good to breathe in fresh air
Every time an executive order is signed

The Biden-Harris administration restored
A state of normal to the art of governance
Without having to explode the intersection
Of hard work and progressive values

We can scan the horizon of a pink morning skyline
And press our feet on solid ground of actual truth
And feel lightness to our being authentically real
And share love to care for our common humanity

Celebrating, "This is the day that the Lord has made
Let us rejoice and be glad in it," an everyday Psalm
So history has consigned mistakes to the past
We can look to the future with dawn in our eyes.

> *1/22/21 (On occasion of reviewing a week of peaceful exchange of power and a call to live nuclear free)*

Acknowledgements

To THE GREAT WORK of Fellow Resisters of Oppression, including the Poor People's Campaign supporting Martin Luther King Jr.'s legacy of non-violent protest against the evils of racism, poverty, militarism, and environmental degradation, as well as those who are calling out the illegal use of nuclear weapons.

To the best collaborators: Henry Stoever, Charles Carney, Bob George, Jonne Avery Long, Cheri Avery Black, Kriss Avery, Bob Francis, Marcia Callis, Dale Shetler, Steve Brew, Earl Atkinson, and spa-peace-church friends.

To my love, Toni B. Faust.

PeaceWorks Kansas City—**2019 Memorial Day protest against nuclear weapons.** *Photo by Jim Hannah.*

About the Author

Ronald L. Faust, BTh, MDiv, DMin, CFLE

REV. DR. RON FAUST works with peace, justice, and ecology groups such as PeaceWorks Kansas City and Disciples Peace Fellowship. He received a Doctor of Ministry from DREW University in Madison, New Jersey; a Master of Divinity from Christian Theological Seminary in Indianapolis, Indiana; and a Bachelor of Theology from Bushnell University (formerly NCC) in Eugene, Oregon. At the center of his circle of love are his wife, Toni; their children, Jeremy and Tuesday; and five grandchildren. He creates poetry under his Gazebo, beside two waterfalls.

Books by the Author

A Cup of Coffee

Prophetic Poetry: A Holy Agitation for Peace, Justice, and Passion

Prophetic Poetry: A Holy Occasion for Peace, Justice, and Ecology

Prophetic Poetry: A Holy Occasion for Openness, Authenticity, and Love

Poems for Lonely Prophets

GAPS

GRAND PARENTING for Compassion and Peace

Five Faces of Love

A Room Full of Shadows

UNPRECEDENTED

www.ingramcontent.com/pod-product-compliance
Lightning Source LLC
Chambersburg PA
CBHW070502100426
42743CB00010B/1733